Our Sun, Our Weather

Table of Contents

Nancy White

Here comes the sun!
As the sun rises, a new day begins.

The sun warms the land,
water, and air.

The sun's warmth also makes our **weather**.

We get information about the weather from **meteorologists**. These scientists **predict** what the weather will be.

| Monday | Tuesday | Wednesday | Thursday | Friday |

Look at this five-day weather **forecast**. Which photograph matches the forecast for each day?

The sun gives us sunny days.

Zion National Park, Utah

In some places, the weather can be very hot. The **temperature** goes way up!

The sun also makes clouds.
The sun's warmth makes water
evaporate into the air as **vapor**.
The water vapor cools and forms
tiny droplets, which become clouds.

Hoh Rain Forest, Washington

When the droplets get big and heavy, they fall to the ground as rain.

In some places, it rains every day.

In very cold
weather, the
droplets freeze.
They fall as
sleet or snow.

Sometimes
snow can be
very deep!

Our weather is always changing. What prediction can you make about the weather in this photograph?

Even on cloudy days, the sun is still there, shining brightly above the clouds.

The sun makes wind, too.
As the sun warms the air,
it causes the air to move.

What is happening on
this windy day?

At the end of each day, the sun sets. The temperature cools. We can see the moon and stars.

In the morning, another day will begin. The sun will warm the land, water, and air.

It will light up our world.

Glossary

evaporate (ih-VAP-uh-rayt): dry up

forecast (FOR-kast): a statement of what will happen

meteorologist (mee-tee-uh-ROL-uh-jist): a scientist who studies, and may forecast, the weather

predict (prih-DIKT): tell what may happen in the future

temperature (TEM-pur-uh-chur): the degree of hotness or coldness of a place

vapor (VAY-pur): water that has dried up and gone into the air

weather (WEH-<u>thur</u>): a day's hotness or coldness, wetness or dryness, calmness or windiness, and clearness or cloudiness

Index